P9-DLZ-585

ADEBAMBO IEYISOPE
OSIFESO

WEEKLY WR READER®
EARLY LEARNING LIBRARY

+ SAFETY FIRST

Staying Safe
At School

by Joanne Mattern

Reading consultant: Susan Nations, M.Ed.,
author/literacy coach/consultant in literacy development

Please visit our web site at: www.garethstevens.com
For a free color catalog describing Weekly Reader® Early Learning Library's list
of high-quality books, call 1-877-445-5824 (USA) or 1-800-387-3178 (Canada).
Weekly Reader® Early Learning Library's fax: (414) 336-0164.

Library of Congress Cataloging-in-Publication Data

Mattern, Joanne, 1963-
    Staying safe at school / by Joanne Mattern.
       p. cm. — (Safety first)
    Includes bibliographical references and index.
    ISBN-13: 978-0-8368-7792-2 (lib. bdg.)
    ISBN-13: 978-0-8368-7799-1 (softcover)
    1. Schools—Safety measures—Juvenile literature. 2. Safety education—Juvenile literature.
    I. Title.
  LB2864.5.M39   2007
  363.11'371—dc22   2006030334

This edition first published in 2007 by
Weekly Reader® Early Learning Library
A Member of the WRC Media Family of Companies
330 West Olive Street, Suite 100
Milwaukee, WI 53212 USA

Copyright © 2007 by Weekly Reader® Early Learning Library

Managing editor: Valerie J. Weber
Editor: Barbara Kiely Miller
Art direction: Tammy West
Cover design and page layout: Charlie Dahl
Picture research: Diane Laska-Swanke
Photographer: Jack Long

All rights reserved. No part of this book may be reproduced, stored in a retrieval system,
or transmitted in any form or by any means, electronic, mechanical, photocopying, recording,
or otherwise, without the prior written permission of the copyright holder.

Printed in the United States of America

1 2 3 4 5 6 7 8 9 10 10 09 08 07 06

Note to Educators and Parents

Reading is such an exciting adventure for young children! They are beginning to integrate their oral language skills with written language. To encourage children along the path to early literacy, books must be colorful, engaging, and interesting; they should invite the young reader to explore both the print and the pictures.

The *Safety First* series is designed to help young readers review basic safety rules, learn new vocabulary, and strengthen their reading comprehension. In simple, easy-to-read language, each book teaches children to stay safe in an everyday situation such as at home, at school, or in the outside world.

Each book is specially designed to support the young reader in the reading process. The familiar topics are appealing to young children and invite them to read — and reread — again and again. The full-color photographs and enhanced text further support the student during the reading process.

In addition to serving as wonderful picture books in schools, libraries, homes, and other places where children learn to love reading, these books are specifically intended to be read within an instructional guided reading group. This small group setting allows beginning readers to work with a fluent adult model as they make meaning from the text. After children develop fluency with the text and content, the book can be read independently. Children and adults alike will find these books supportive, engaging, and fun!

— Susan Nations, M.Ed., author, literacy coach,
and consultant in literacy development

Do you know how to stay safe at school?

Do not run in the halls. Stay in line and do not push.

Be careful when you carry things. Carry scissors with the sharp end pointing down.

A **fire drill** lets you **practice** how to get out of school safely if there is a fire. Listen for the **alarm**.

During a fire drill, you must leave the school. Do not run or talk.

Follow the rules at **recess**. Wait for your turn. Watch out for other children playing.

Tell a teacher if someone gets hurt. The school nurse will help.

Some children might try to hurt others. These children are called **bullies**. Tell a teacher if someone is acting like a bully.

Everyone at school works together to make school a safe place!

Glossary

alarm — a sound, light, or other signal that warns people about danger

bullies — people who are mean to other people or who try to hurt them

fire drill — the practice of the right way to get out of a building in case of a fire

practice — to repeat something many times so you can get better at it

recess — a short time to rest or play during the day

For More Information

Books

A Fire Drill with Mr. Dill. Read-It! Readers (series). Susan Blackaby (Picture Window Books)

Learning How to Stay Safe at School. The Violence Prevention Library (series). Susan Kent (PowerKids Press)

School Safety. Living Well, Safety (series). Lucia Raatma (Child's World)

Who's Who in a School Community. Communities at Work (series). Jake Miller (PowerKids Press)

Web Sites

Milstein Child Safety Center

www.mcgruff.org

McGruff the Crime Dog shows you how to deal with bullies.

Hi, I'm Michael!

www.chp.edu/besafe/cartoons/playground_lbw.swf

Let Michael show you the rules for playground safety.

Publisher's note to educators and parents: Our editors have carefully reviewed these Web sites to ensure that they are suitable for children. Many Web sites change frequently, however, and we cannot guarantee that a site's future contents will continue to meet our high standards of quality and educational value. Be advised that children should be closely supervised whenever they access the Internet.

23

Index

About the Author

Joanne Mattern has written more than 150 books for children. She has written about weird animals, sports, world cities, dinosaurs, and many other subjects. Joanne also works in her local library. She lives in New York State with her husband, three daughters, and assorted pets. She enjoys animals, music, going to baseball games, reading, and visiting schools to talk about her books.